For
The Imperfect Parent 111
Perfect Parenting Quotes

By Kidsstoppress.com

ISBN 979-8-88883-615-6

Author's Note

No one said parenting is easy. It comes with its own set of insecurities, emotions and frustrations and days when you feel "you have done nothing right!" The fact that we give it our best every day, love them unconditionally and still have these doubts is just crazy. Breathe. We are all in this together.

I now know that being a good parent doesn't mean you have to be perfect. It means being real, being strong and rolling with the fun times even though there are days when they drive you absolutely crazy.

I have had my days when I thought I did things wrong, when I doubted myself and felt like I needed that push from the universe to tell me that "it is okay". This book is an effort to give you that invisible push. That pat on the back. And a shoulder to cry on.

It is a compilation of our efforts over a period of time, that you have 'liked' and 'shared' on Instagram. I have had so many parents reach out in DMs and WhatsApp saying "you read my mood exactly!" or " I just needed this today!" That's what this book is

#simplifyingparenting

about- to show you that we are in this together. As a fraternity.

Go ahead, read this on a day you feel happy. Read this on a day you feel not so good. Re-read them on days to know that you are not alone. And gift it to a fellow parent to show them you have their back.

This book along with others makes for a great present for new parents, a quick read for current parents, or a coffee-table conversation starter. If there's one thing I can promise it is you can pick it up or gift this to a parent with a child of any age. Parenting jokes are forever.

This book is 1 of 3 in our series of Parenting. The other two are doses of moments that you will need when you want to lighten the mood with some humour and pep talks when you want to share a problem or just about give up but you can't. Yes, we all have those days. We're here to get you through it all. Share your favourite quotes as you go through the book. We are just a handle away @kidsstoppress and @mansi.zaveri.

We hope you enjoy it as much as we have loved putting it together.

XOXO,
Mansi Zaveri

For
The Imperfect Parent 111
Perfect Parenting Quotes

By Kidsstoppress.com

1

To all the parents who get smothered with kisses and hugs. Enjoy them. They will not be yours forever.

———

2

Your kids will remember the adventures you went on, not the stuff you've bought them. Kids outgrow stuff, they never outgrow adventures.

———

3

Parenting is the easiest thing in the world to have an opinion about, but the hardest thing in the world to do.

———

4

Your child is a wonderful being & you are getting the honour of seeing them bloom into their best versions. Enjoy it.

———

5

Your child is not your report
card for being the best parent.

———

6

Don't resent your partner
for not understanding what
you're going through. Your
and your partner's journey is
different and everyone copes
with it differently. Focus on the
positives and you are going to
love every aspect of parenting.

———

7

Say NO, when you need to.
You are just being kind to
yourself and not selfish.

———

8

You don't owe anybody an explanation. You are the best mother to your kids no matter what.

———

9

If you did nothing besides hugging your kids today... You have done enough.

———

10

You are not selfish if you want alone time.

———

11

Not loving every moment of motherhood doesn't mean you don't love being a mom.

———

12

You are still a strong parent if you get overwhelmed and cry in front of your kids. You are showing them that being vulnerable is not shameful and should be expressed.

———

13

How many people in the world have the privilege of being called Mom/Dad/Parents?

______

#KSP

quotes

14

You are still a good parent
even if you lose your cool
sometimes.

———

15

You have to think about everyone and everything. But don't forget to think about yourself too.

——

16

You always put everyone before yourself. Sometimes it's okay to put yourself before others.

———

17

Don't let that voice in your head criticize your body. Your body created life itself and that's something to cherish. You're beautiful and strong no matter what!

———

#youare

thebest

18

Remind yourself that you go beyond managing schedules and meal plans. You are a person with needs, wants and dreams too. Stop seeking for validation to love yourself. You deserve it.

———

19

You are doing more than enough by simply existing and loving your kids and your family.

———

20

You can be sad and thankful
just like you can be full and
still eat some cake.

———

21

When I was a kid, my mom was the last one to leave the house, sometimes even running back in and it seemed like forever. I would wonder what was she doing. Now I get it.

———

22

I need to understand that my kid needing me less doesn't mean they love me less.

———

23

My child didn't make it to the first few ranks to captaincy but stopped to help a friend who fell down while running in a competitive race, compromising her chances to the gold. Feels like I am doing something right.

———

#simplifyingparenting

24

Try to always see the best in your kids, especially when they cannot see it in themselves.

———

25

Raising kids is not a compromise to my being. It's evolution of me as a being.

———

26

It's easy to lose ourselves in our daily chores and responsibilities. But remind yourself that you are more than just the work you do.

———

27

Don't let that voice inside your head stop you from dreaming big. There's nothing you cannot achieve.

———

#blessedto

beaparent

28

Let's Replace:
I want to protect my child
from tough feelings with
I want to prepare my child for
tough feelings.

______

29

There is no formula to raising kids. You just hug them when they let you.

———

30

Your kids won't tell you everything that happened at school. When they do, listen to them with a patient ear and undivided attention.

———

31

Yes, we want to yell at our kids sometimes. Reminder. That's not why we had them.

———

32

Say NO to situations you are
not comfortable with.

___

33

There is no one lonelier than parents who have dropped their kids to university and opened the door to their child's room 10 times a day.

____

34

You have only 16 summers
(0 – 16 years) with your kids.
Make each one of them count.

———

35

Stop saying "I am a mess" instead say "I am good inside even when there is a mess on the outside."

———

36

In times you feel you are doing everything wrong, remind yourself, you are doing the best you can. And that's great.

———

37

Your kids love you inspite of

- Your fine lines
- Stretch marks
- Saggy boobs
- Bulging curves
- Fat thighs

They haven't noticed all that
at all.

———

38

One day:
The laundry basket won't be overflowing,
Your calendar won't say sports days and PTM's,
There will be no science test to prep for,
There won't be grunting sounds like Peppa all around your house,
And that day you will know that someone is all grown up and doesn't need you as much anymore.

———

39

Trust your kids and have faith in them. Only then will they trust and have faith in themselves.

———

40

Some of the most
well-rounded, grounded kids
I know are being raised in
houses that are messy, by
parents who forget practices,
serve frozen pizza for dinner
and can't afford to buy them
branded clothes.

______

41

Say no to situations you are not comfortable with. It's okay to not be the one always adjusting.

———

#mynam

eismama

42

Whenever you start to feel like you're not good enough, just look at your child. You created that beautiful, happy, energy-sucking, little being. Way to go mama!

———

43

It's not difficult to take care
of a child, it's difficult to do
anything else while taking care
of a child.

———

44

It's OK for moms putting themselves first. It's also OK that moms don't have to do it all, even when they can.

———

45

The best thing that being a parent has taught me is to love someone more than myself.

———

90% of the scenarios
you blame yourself for, were
never in your control anyway.
Let it go.

———

47

Parenting is the easiest thing in the world to have an opinion about, but the hardest thing in the world to do.

———

48

There are hard days in motherhood, but looking at your baby sleeping reminds you why it's all worth it.

———

49

There will be many times in your life that you hug your child, knowing you needed that hug more than they did.

50

I am not going to blame my children everytime I lose my cool. If they knew what they were doing, we wouldn't be 30 years apart.

———

51

Don't ever compare yourself to other mothers. We are all losing our shit. Some just hide it better than others.

———

52

You don't need to have a perfect house, be a perfect parent or dish out big bucks to raise awesome kids. You just need to be there when they need you.

———

53

Perfect moms don't exist. The right time to have a baby doesn't exist. The right number of children doesn't exist. Stop waiting for perfection and let's focus on happiness instead.

———

54

When you're feeling like you're not cut out for this, just remember: You were hand-picked to be their parent.

———

55

Every time you say YES to your dreams and ambitions doesn't mean you are saying NO to your child.

———

Dear Dad, Thanks for always saying YES when mom said NO.

———

57

Mama, you may feel like you're failing. But when I look at you, all I see is love.

———

#littlean

dbrave

58

What motherhood has taught me is that I can't be everything for everyone.

———

59

Spending money on yourself
does not make you greedy.

———

60

Your dreams become achievable the moment you start believing them. Practice this and your kids will too.

———

61

I support another mom's struggles, tears and smiles because I am not her and she is not me. We are both doing the best we can with the cards we've been dealt!

———

62

My child's admission to the "right school" neither defines me as a parent nor my child's ability to be happy.

———

63

All my life's problems have just one simple solution. A hug from my child.

64

One generation of deeply loving parents would change the brain of the next generation, and with that, the world.

————

65

It's a gift to our kids when they
see us value ourselves and
pursue our passions.

———

#livethelit

tlethings

66

Being a parent isn't all black and white. You can be a total mess but still be a good parent. You're allowed to be both.

———

67

Hey Mom/Dad, in case no one has told you this week...I see you making hard decisions. I see you doing hard things. I see you being a great parent. You are strong!

———

68

Don't let motherhood steal the spotlight from the many roles you play as a woman.

———

69

Treat yourself the way you treat every person in your life – with dignity, respect, love and care.

______

70

Consistency is harder when no one is clapping for you. You must clap for yourself during those times. Be your biggest fan.

———

71

Yes, I like my wine. Yes, I like being fit. Yes, I help my kids with their homework. Yes, I'm cool. Yes, I am a Mom Boss! Any more questions?

———

72

Don't be afraid to tell your kids how proud you are of them and it's okay to make mistakes too.

———

73

Instead of buying your kids everything you never had, teach them everything you were never taught.

———

#simplifyingparenting

74

Parenting is much easier for us when we choose to be on our own side instead of in our own way.

———

75

It's not wrong to be passionate about your career. When you love what you do, you bring that stimulation back to your family.

———

76

Trust your parenting instincts more than external voices.

———

77

Why don't kids come with user manuals and pause buttons?

———

78

Stop expecting your kids
to chase their dreams,
respect themselves, forgive
themselves, love themselves...
if they spent a lifetime
watching you do the opposite
for yourself.

———

79

I've run out of patience with people who make parenthood a competition. Be the village. Not the villain.

———

80

The first rule for your kids respecting you is to respect yourself.

———

81

Your current parenting style
is perfectly aligned to the
current reality. Let that sink in.

———

82

Don't say, "What did I do today?" Make a list of things that you did and wonder who else could do it.

———

83

Dads make good moms too.

———

#simplifyingparenting

84

I created this child and this child is special. This child is unique. When we respect that uniqueness, we respect creation. In that respect lies a lot of satisfaction.

———

85

I am a mom. I am far from perfect. I make mistakes and I lose my shit often. But that is okay. No one could love my children more than me.

———

#magicof

childhood

86

You can be a mess and still be a good parent. We are allowed to be both.

———

87

I know stay-at-home moms and I know career moms. But I have yet to meet a mom who doesn't work.

———

88

Be present. Not perfect.

———

89

Right now is not your forever.

———

90

There's a lot our moms don't tell us and we only realize that when we have our own children.

———

91

You cannot raise your children as your parents raised you, because your parents raised you for a world that no longer exists.

———

92

Trust your instincts because you have most of the answers.

———

93

The reason I need me-time is
so that I can be fully present
for my children.

———

94

As a mother, you have to get to a point where your mood doesn't shift based on the insignificant actions of others.

———

95

It's ok if you fall apart as a parent sometimes. Tacos fall apart and we still love them.

———

96

It's important to recognise when to take time off for yourself so you can be a happy parent. That's all that matters.

———

97

We have been trying for generations but the concept of a 'perfect parent' just doesn't exist! So, don't bog yourself down.

———

98

Stop doubting yourself. Your kids are watching you. Dream big and know you are the best parent to them.

99

Let your kids spread their wings and dream. Don't try and mould them to be what you want.

———

100

We need to teach our kids that grades don't reflect our capability but is the outcome of our hard work and the efforts put behind it. The thin line that separates the good from the rest is the excellence that we need to strive for.

———

101

You are the biggest and
most important cheerleader
for your kids.

———

102

When you feel like your teenager is pushing you away or is changing every day, remember, they are simply trying stuff on– friends, personalities, fashion, hobbies to see what fits them the best. Make sure they know you love them no matter what version they're showing you that day!

———

103

I wish I understood earlier that my kids needing me less, doesn't mean they don't love me. They need to figure out where they fit in the world and I need to trust that when they figure it out they will be back and know that we're there waiting for them.

———

#simplifyingparenting

104

'What's your favourite childhood memory?' I asked my little one. 'Falling asleep on the sofa & waking up in your bed snuggled up to you'. Complete heart melt moment!

———

105

There are no bad kids. Just impressionable conflicted young people wrestling with emotions & impulses trying to communicate their feelings and it's the only way they know how.

——

106

Children are never good at listening to us but they never fail to imitate us. So, tread carefully.

———

107

If you walk into my house
and hear yelling. Well! It's
not yelling. It is motivational
speaking for people who don't
want to listen.

———

108

The sign of great parenting is not the child's behaviour. The sign of truly great parenting is the parent's behaviour.

———

109

Being kind to yourself isn't about ignoring your weaknesses, it's about accepting your flaws and learning from your mistakes.

———

110

One day you're gonna remember the days you felt like a complete disaster of a parent and be proud of growing through it.

———

111

Life is made up of memories. Don't go wasting it with careless worries.

———

#Thanks

@mommy_unsensored

@KaraFerwerda

@mindful_madre

@HeidiPowell

@kissesfromboys

@raisingteenstoday

Some of these quotes are inspired from fellow parents and most are from our real-life experiences.

We thank all parents for sharing their thoughts with the world.

Disclaimer: In case we missed giving you credit, it was not intentional. We were unable to find the sources of some of our favourite quotes.

#myfavouritequotes

While we wish our memories could keep track of all our favourites, write down your special quotes so you can keep track of them all.

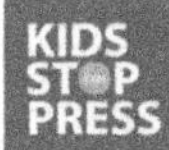

While we wish our memories could keep track of all our favourites, write down your special quotes so you can keep track of them all.

While we wish our memories could keep track of all our favourites, write down your special quotes so you can keep track of them all.

Team Credit

This book is a compilation of our efforts over a period of time, that you have 'liked' and 'shared' on Instagram. I have had so many moms reach out in DMs and WhatsApp saying "you read my mood exactly!" or " I just needed this today!"

We would like to thank all those who have worked extremely hard to make the 111 Perfect Parenting Quotes For The Imperfect Parent book possible.

Mansi Zaveri for her drive, vision and passion. She's been the mentor we needed to drive this through. Without her unconditional support and constant encouragement this book would not have been possible.

Parul Gupta for being the steady anchor we always need for projects like this.. As a teen parent she needs a lot of laughter & tons of positive energy and through this book she's helped bring it to you too.

Tanya Lemos for her patience, the constant follow ups and for all the never ending changes we have been making to make this book perfect for you. Her calm and composure has been a great help in making sure this book delivered all that we promised.